Robin Sees a Monster

From Egg to Robin

Barbara A. Fanson

Published by Sterling Education Centre Inc.
More activities on our website: http://fanson.net

Dedicated to Kathleen Malaraczuk
for her inspiration and ideas.

And to my personal consultant Kristen Van Kampen
who helped create the expression: robin deflector noggin protector.

The date at the bottom of each page is the date the photograph was taken.

Author and graphic designer Barbara Fanson wrote *Shirl the Squirrel Rises to New Heights*, a children's picture book and *Tragedy on the Twenty*, a historical fiction book. She has also written over 30 non-fiction books including *Milestones & Memories, Preserving Smithville, Illustrator One Step at a Time, Start & Run a Desktop Publishing Business,* and *Producing a First-Class Newsletter.*

She lives in Hamilton, Ontario with a dashing black cat, 7 squirrels, 2 robins, a rabbit, and her human family.

She used 21 point Avenir for the body text because it has a regular "g."

Photographs were taken by the author; thank you Pixabay.com for the photo of the photographer with camera.

Robin Sees a Monster
From Egg to Robin

Published by Sterling Education Centre Inc.
http://fanson.net

Get more activity sheets from our website: http://fanson.net

Thank you for reading. If you have a moment, please post a review on Amazon, Goodreads or Kirkus Reviews. Thank you.

Copyright © 2019 Barbara A. Fanson. All Rights Reserved.
Book ISBN: 978-1-989361-04-7   Electronic ISBN: 978-1-989361-03-0

No part of this publication may be reproduced or stored in a retrieval system, or transmitted in any form or by any means, electronic, mechanical, recording, or otherwise, without writ-ten permission of the publisher:

Sterling Education Centre Inc.
220 Homebrook Drive, Mount Hope, ON
Canada L0R 1W0

Email: learn@sterlinged.com   Telephone: (905) 679-9229

Robin had just returned from her vacation down south. She knew she had to make a nest.

Robin carried some dry weeds to the top of a hydro box on the side of a house.

April 22

Robin had a nest there last year and she liked the neighborhood. There was plenty of food for her and her babies, dry weeds to make a nest, and mud to hold the nest together.

April 22

The wind blew and a weed fell to the ground. Robin flew down, picked up the weed in her beak, and flew it back to the hydro box. Robin knew she had to work quickly on that windy day.

April 22

Robin found a puddle nearby with wet gooey mud.

She added some mud to hold the weeds together. Robin built a nest in one day.

April 22

The very next day, Robin laid a light blue egg in the nest. It was robin egg blue.

April 23

Robin laid another blue egg. And then another. And another. Then, there were four.

Robins usually lay 3, 4, or 5 eggs per nesting. They may have up to 3 clutches or batches per year.

April 24

For 14 days, Robin sat on the eggs to keep them warm.

One day, a monster appeared holding a gadget. She pointed it right at Robin.

April 29

Robin stared at the monster. She tweeted loudly and finally, the monster left.

One day, Robin heard a sound … the sound of an egg hatching! She got up to see a small hole in one egg. The baby bird inside kept pecking on the egg shell to get it to open.

May 12

The egg broke and a baby bird crawled out exhausted. The baby bird's eyes were closed and it had no feathers.

Each of the eggs hatched and a baby robin crawled out.

After the eggs hatched, Robin picked up the eggshells in her beak and flew over to a nearby park.

She dropped the shells in the middle of the grass field far away from any trees so that if a predator, like a cat or raccoon smelled the shells, it would not find her nest.

The monster returned with the gadget in her hands and aimed it at Robin. The monster shot the robin with the gadget!

"Go away," she tweeted.

May 16

"Get away from my babies!" tweeted Robin as she flew at the head of the monster. Finally, the monster left.

a robin deflector noggin protector

The next day, the monster came back wearing a robin deflector noggin protector.

She aimed the gadget at Robin, who was sitting on a roof near the nest.

"Go away!" tweeted the mama bird.

May 16

Robin tweeted several times to distract the monster, but the monster did not move. Robin dove at the monster but hit the robin deflector noggin protector. It was hard, but finally the monster left.

Robin checked her baby birds, which are also called chicks. They were fine.

May 15

The baby robins still had their eyes closed, but they could eat the food Robin brought.

The male and female robin took turns bringing grubs, worms, caterpillars, insects, and fruit to the baby chicks.

Robins have very good eyesight and can see if the ground is moving slightly. If an earthworm is near the surface, a robin will scoop him out right away.

May 16

When a robin approaches, the baby chicks open their beaks.

Robin places food into their mouths.

May 16

The baby birds are now 6 days old and starting to look like robins. Soft feathers have started to grow on the chicks.

May 18

Robin spotted a cat eating grass nearby. The cat heard a peep. He looked up to see where the sound was coming from.

It sounds like a baby bird … a delicious baby bird.

The black cat crept towards the nest.

Robin saw the cat coming and tweeted to distract him.

Robin attacked the black cat with her feet and tweeted loudly.

The cat ran away.

Robin flew back to the nest to check her babies. She knew they were not safe and should learn to fly soon. The baby chicks have their eyes open now.

May 21

The baby robins are now 8 days old. They usually fly away from the nest when they are about 14 days old.

Robin continued to bring insects and worms to the young birds.

May 21

The baby birds are 10 days old now.

The four birds have grown quickly and are crowded in the nest.

May 22

The wings on the young birds are **growing** and they have more feathers. Notice the white bird droppings on the wall and the nest.

May 23

The next day, one young bird flew down to the fence.

He is 14 days old. When baby chicks have feathers and are ready to fly, they are called fledglings.

Another fledgling flew to the wood rail on the deck. He will stay near the nest until he grows tail feathers and is strong enough to fly.

May 26

Robin has more food for her babies, but she found the young birds had already flown the coop.

Discussion

Robins can be found everywhere on Earth, but each continent has its own robin. In the United States and Canada, American Robins fly south during winter, but European Robins puff up their feathers to insulate its body against cold winds.

Most robins have a red breast, grey under wings and tail feathers, brown head, wings, and tail. They fly fast, but short flights.

1. Have you seen an American Robin hopping on the grass? _____
2. Have you ever seen a bird's nest? _____
3. What can you do to attract robins? _____
4. When a female robin lays eggs, does the male robin hang around? _____
5. How many eggs does a robin usually lay? _____
6. How many times a year can a robin lay eggs? _____
7. Unfortunately, robins have a short lifespan. Almost 75% of robins will die within one year. Can you list 3 causes of death: _____
8. What is the difference between a robin's nest and other bird's nest? _____
9. What is the difference between a squirrel's nest and a bird's nest? _____

Answers:

3. Dig in the garden or flowerbed and you will see robins perched in trees nearby hoping to get an earthworm. Or, turn on your water sprinkler or put fresh water in a birdbath so birds can clean their wings to make flying easier.
4. Yes, the male robin hangs around until the baby birds leave the nest. He will bring the female robin worms and caterpillars while she sits on the eggs. When the eggs hatch, the male and female robin bring lunch to the baby birds.
5. A robin usually lays 3 to 5 eggs each time.
6. A female robin can lay up to 3 batches of eggs per year.
7. Predators such as raccoons, cats, dogs, and squirrels can attack a nest of baby birds. Robins may die defending their territory from other robins or they can't fend for themselves.
8. A robin uses mud to mold the nest into a bowl and hold the dried weeds together. Other birds don't use mud; their nests have loose dried weeds.
9. A squirrel gathers leaves into a large pile.

From Egg to Robin

A robin's egg will hatch in about 14 days and then leave the nest in about 14 days.

www.ingramcontent.com/pod-product-compliance
Lightning Source LLC
Chambersburg PA
CBHW040005080526
44586CB00027B/2892